THE JOY
OF
SACRIFICE

Keys to Inner Transformation

WRITTEN & ILLUSTRATED BY
E.J. Gold

Gateways Books and Tapes
Nevada City, California

Second Edition © 2023 by E.J. Gold
ISBN: 978-0-89556-262-3 (Trade Paperback)
        978-0-89556-676-8 (Digital & eBook editions)
Previously published by IDHHB Publishing
First Edition 1978 / ISBN: 0-89556-003-8
LCCN: 78-54140
Some material herein appeared previously under the title:
The Book of Sacrifices, © 1974 by E.J. Gold

Illustrations © 2023 by E.J. Gold
Series: Gods and Goddesses Take a Selfie
Note: After a distinguished career of more than 50 years as a sculptor, graphic artist, painter, and game designer, E.J. Gold has embarked on a new art experiment in collaboration with AI artistry. The present series was created using the Night Café program, a text to image AI generator.

Layout and cover design: Gailyn Porter
Proofreading: Tabatha Jones

THE JOY OF SACRIFICE

Table of Contents   page   #

THE LETTERS

God takes a selfie

Mezar-e-Chariff, 4 August

Dear Ones, Beloved of God:

I hope this letter finds you in the best of health and well on your way toward taking an active part in the Work. We here wish with all our beings for each of you to succeed in this Great Aim.

Allow me now to explain to you some ideas about the beginning stages of your work to help meet the obligation of a human being for the fulfillment of God's plan for human beings of the planet Earth.

As you are already aware, the appearance on Earth of the race of humans is a crucial event in the life of the Universe. The act of being human is a necessary and important stage in the evolution of a planet...And more importantly to you, in the personal evolution of the being.

It allows us to actively participate in self-evolution by fusing the intellectual, emotional and physical centers into a single unified presence through the process of intentional suffering; to perfect ourselves through conscious labors; and to attain crystallization of the soul through the process of the collection and transformation of higher substances.

To be human is a sanctification not possible in any other form. Human beings have the unique property of being potentially able to make the special conscious efforts necessary to help God.

Because of this unique property, we have the chance to perfect ourselves automatically, through the means of taking upon ourselves a special obligation.

The human lifespan is abnormally shortened compared to what it could be. Scientists today wonder how "primitive savages" were able to live very long lives without the so-called benefits of modern medicine.

Until recently human beings lived normal lives for the organism, which was placed under continual tension and stress, thus developing the essence automatically by preventing the formation of personality, which can only function under extreme low-voltage conditions of the nervous system. Stress produces high voltages, forcing the essence to operate the organism.

At the same time, life was much simpler, allowing one to maintain oneself internally without the need for externals demanded by today's mechanical culture. Now all this has changed, and life no longer presents the stress and simplicity it once did...And if by accident it happens to, why, there is always some pill or other one can take to make it go away...That stress which was in ancient times called Alchemical Fire.

Today these factors are not found in nature, and in a school we are constrained to introduce them artificially. But in this comfort-oriented, labor-saving civilization there are very few who wish actively for a life of stress and friction for themselves, when they can simply slide through life just "getting by".

Under conditions normal for a human being, the continual state of tensions keeps the individual at least in the organic sense, awake. Through practices of self-calming, stress is dissipated, thus allowing the individual to plow himself even more deeply into sleep.

The lifespan and experience of a human being can be quite long; subjectively many thousands of years, even though the organism is now limited to a span of sixty or seventy years objective time. On the other hand, the lifespan of the psyche is only as long as each "mask", or "posture" is in control of the organism...Usually about fifteen seconds. This is not sufficient time to accomplish anything, much less the processes of the collection of higher substances, and their perfection and crystallization into a real soul.

The essence was intended to experience life in an unbroken chain of consciousness, regardless of variations in situation, state or organic conditions.

Thus one was intended to experience the movement from one formation of the psyche to another without losing the connecting thread of consciousness.

It is true that there are many practices which seem to offer salvation, but in reality only man can redeem himself. One is indeed deep in the trap of vanity if he believes that his sacrifices have already been made for him. Messengers from Above have manifested not to save others, but to show them how to achieve their own redemption.

We can remain alive long enough to achieve redemption only if we are able to endure the journey through the abyss which lies between the outer self, personality and the deep self, essence.

One can learn to live alone, to be alone, even to work alone, but one cannot endure the corridor of madness without help of some kind. This special help is the true function of a school.

A school does not take advantage of the superstitions existing commonly among men, nor does it play upon the fears and beliefs surrounding survival. It does not trade services for material considerations, and its teaching cannot be bought at any price. It remains neither hidden or exposed, neither available to the general public nor unreachable by those in need of a school. It is an entity unto itself, existing completely apart from the outer world.

How is it that so few seek help from a school? Why is it that most people choose the path of sleep, passion, gratification, pleasure and power, and so few choose the path of transformation? Why is the pursuit of man a necessary function of God?

You yourselves have seen the children born into the Work. You have heard them discourse and teach the elders. You have seen with your own eyes that a continuous state of unbroken consciousness is possible and that a few communities have maintained this method throughout human history in spite of all the destructive actions of ordinary man.

I recently had the opportunity to introduce these ideas into the lives of several people here. When they learned that it was simply a matter of regaining something lost by contemporary man, and not something unusual for man, they wondered why resistance is so strong. I explained to them that in order to bring man back to the state in which he is man without quotation marks, everything must be just right; all conditions must be met exactly. This is impossible while man believes himself to be presently operating at his full potential.

To prepare for the work the psyche must be developed to some degree, but not crystallized. The essence must still be alive. The individual must be capable of learning hand crafts and other manual skills. The personality must be fluid, not fixated beyond change. Most of all, one must be able to ask for help and able to accept it when it is given.

Most of these factors are quite beyond the reach of ordinary man. Thus there are very few who are able to come to the school as a result of inner self-created barriers.

Soon it will be a time to awaken the teaching in the West. Each shall have its turn. The life of man will once again be as it was meant to be, and he will fulfill his objective aim and purpose for existence. Thus was it written, and thus shall it be manifested.

Brahman takes a selfie

Jerusalem, 22 November

Dear Ones, Beloved of God:

Much has been left unsaid about the science of sacrifices and their necessity in the Work and as preparation for Work. I will send as much data by post as possible, and then we shall work together when we see each other.

Sacrifices may seem silly, unnecessary, perhaps even masochistic to the Westerner when he encounters these ideas for the first time without the usual trappings of mystical materialism.

I do not ask that you believe, but that you faithfully carry out those experiments indicated by me for elucidation on this subject.

Nothing can be accomplished without sacrifices. If not for the possibility of sacrifice we could not attain conscious life. Do not allow these ideas to frighten you. Try to learn what is meant by sacrifice, rather than trusting to previous data about suffering and sacrifice in the ordinary way.

Sacrifices are very fierce weapons against sleep and its ally, self-love, but on the other end of that stick one can easily grow to like – even to cherish – one's Sacrifices.

The first time it may cause a small awakening, but the second time it has already become tolerable, and by the third time one may have become hardened to it. After a while of performing the same sacrifice one can become enamored of it, growing to prefer it over the way it was before. So it is that we must be beware of mechanicality developing in the path of sacrifices.

One must be ever-alert and continually watchful for changes in one's feelings and attitudes about one's present work. One must not grow to love one's sacrifices as a young child depends upon its mother for milk.

This is a dangerous path, and one must not take it lightly that there are pitfalls. Through sacrifices and special efforts one may come to the doorway of the corridor of madness, and once entered it cannot be escaped by retracing one's steps. Only at the far end is one able to leave it.

To counteract the dangers one has the chance to work in a school. But even with this help the danger is present. In order to minimize this danger, one must be self-honest and able to observe oneself impartially. The teacher can warn you if you are beginning to love your sacrifices, even if you have trouble seeing this for yourself.

Obligation is a thankless task. Very few individuals in this world will appreciate your efforts, and even after years of striving you may not be able to impart what you have learned to others for their benefit.

Your devotion, your efforts and your constant and unfailing sacrifices for the common good will go unheeded in Heaven and on Earth.

You must not perform these obligations with the expectation of reward or merit. The Work is its own reward for those with conscience. In the Work one receives his reward from the moment in which he takes action and is present. Humanity cares nothing for your efforts, and in fact will not only do nothing to assist you in carrying them out, but will, through ignorance and fear, try to destroy you and your work. Even this reaction, when and if it occurs, must become food for your being. It must be understood and accepted.

Hera takes a selfie

Bukhara, 25 November

Beloved of God:

Again I write to you of sacrifices. It seems as if there is much to say on the subject, and yet it is all so simple.

Your sacrifices must have their manifestation according to your station, is it not so?

We must again approach this idea of sacrifices. Not the sacrifices you are accustomed to in ordinary life, nor those you will ultimately make to alleviate the suffering of God, should you succeed in becoming part of the Work. Of course this sacrifice is not possible until all personal and essence sacrifices have been performed.

Sacrifices made in the wrong way at the wrong time result in no real change in being.

Sacrifices must be performed according to law. They must be made in the correct sequence and in the right way.

Each sacrifice stands on the pillars of those sacrifices which have come before it. Each is a doorway which cannot be entered until the doorways leading to it have each been passed in their turn. Thus one can only come face to face with a sacrifice at the exact point when one has that which may be sacrificed.

This is the science of idiotism in its original form, taking one deeper and deeper into essence being. It will lead one to the brink of personal ruin and terror undreamed-of, but beyond all this is the path, after all the tests have been passed. In this state, one is ultimately alone, even though a guide may be with one.

Anubis takes a selfie

Montreal, 29 November

Dear Beloved of God:

I hear that you wish further explanations about sacrifices, and realizing just how important explanations are in your world, I will comply with this wish of yours, of course within certain limits.

To make the first sacrifice, numbered zero, the Sacrifice of Peace of Mind, one need do nothing, and indeed one can do nothing. One is at this stage incapable of making efforts of any kind, and so this sacrifice is made for one by those already in the Work, through direct and indirect influences.

Just by hearing these ideas one's peace of mind is sacrificed. One can never rest quite so easily again as before. By studying the ideas one makes the initial efforts which form a prelude to real work. Simply by allowing yourself to come under the influence of the ideas you have taken the first step on the Hazardous Journey.

In order to make the succeeding sacrifices it is necessary to intentionally choose the path of struggle, to place oneself into certain conditions not at all pleasant for the personality. In beginning group work you will be able to observe how conditions for work are arranged, and how barriers form themselves in one's path to either make one strong or to eliminate those who cannot complete the journey due to personal weaknesses.

The arrangement of such conditions and the orchestration of people within these conditions is beyond even science. It is an art given only at need to those who can best fulfill the function.

How can one bring oneself to make the first self-initiated sacrifice, that of comfort? One can work in a group, and in this way the group can serve as one's work will until one has a will of one's own.

Without organization no real effort is possible for a beginner. Only later will one be able to make efforts on the scale necessary for a genuine effect on being. In the meantime one can learn to harness the inner energies which make work possible, and this can best be learned in a group.

One begins in a small group which in turn is connected to a community of other such groups. Even though these groups may have no direct contact with each other, they are connected through the center of gravity of the school and through the teacher. Each group works along different lines during the preparatory stage, but later they all work in the same way.

A group is not organized along the personal wishes or preferences of its members, but according to the types of individuals placed within it by the teacher and their needs in preparation as "candidates for the Work". The teacher forms a group by placing those individuals together who automatically make continual tensions between themselves, and at the same time wish sincerely to help each other attain the common aim of the group.

Only in such a crucible can the teacher create the alchemical fire which can fuse the centers into a unified being.

In a group effort the teacher selects only those who can genuinely be useful to each other, to themselves, to the teacher and ultimately to the Work.

A group is not just a collection of people with similar interests. It is a formal agreement to work together. All members of the group take a serious oath to help each other struggle against themselves. The teacher accepts only those it is within his power to help. He must refuse pupils who cannot work with him or who have insurmountable inner and outer obstacles.

In order to work in a school one must be able to decide with the whole of one's being to surrender oneself to the school discipline.

Only a person's right attitudes about the Work, the school, the teacher and one's fellow pupils can create the right inner conditions for work on oneself.

In a group nothing is ever given in completed form. One must make efforts to put together those fragments which have been revealed to him and to his fellow students at one time or another. In this way, one is forced to cooperate even with those for whom he has an essence-dislike.

In the struggle against personality the teacher gives the pupil difficult tasks, each more difficult than the last.

Once the first barrier has been overcome, one cannot return to ordinary life even if one wishes to do so, because someone is now occupying one's seat. This first barrier seems impossible to surmount until after it has been transcended. This is why the first barrier is also called the last.

Merytaten takes a selfie

Benares, 3 December

Dear Beloveds of God:

Only if one achieves something real within oneself can it be used as a sacrifice. You ask whether it is possible for you to begin sacrifices now. You must understand that is tis impossible to empty your hands before they hold something. This is why preparation is necessary. To make a genuine sacrifice, not just imaginary, is a very advanced stage. Can you see how this is so?

Remember that real ferocity of purpose is in the inner world, not in a display of odd behavior or dramatic self-flagellation. It is time now to learn the depths of ferocity without the outer show of power and noise.

Ramses takes a selfie

New Delhi, 5 December

Dear Ones:

May this letter find you in your work steadfast and true to your aim. I wish here to give some indications in answer to your questions regarding the newborn.

As one guides a being back into the world one must be aware of the continuity of that individual's consciousness. At the same time one may ignore continuity of identity unless it is that of the essence.

So that the lifespan continues in an unbroken chain, there are several practices which may be useful. We will discuss these in group work. At the end of the Corridor of Madness the psyche has been broken down and dispersed. But if essence cannot assume responsibility for the organism, the psyche re-forms once again into its old habitual pattern. Thus one may be worse off than before unless preparation has been made for this event.

Great care must be taken for the reborn. Essence must be kept awake and the first impressions must be carefully maintained to give all possible types of impressions to the newly born. This must be continued at least for the first year following rebirth of the essence.

During all states between entry and exit in the corridor, one guides by focusing on that which is eternal in the being, not on that which is not his own.

One cannot teach another in the corridor – one can only guide. One should remain calm and centered during this service, either at the bedside of the dying psyche or in the birthing chamber of the reborn essence. Your calm center will be all the help required if fusion has occurred successfully. One should be ready to offer help to one who is ready for it, but must not inflict freedom on those who love their slavery.

Krishna takes a selfie

Luzon, 25 December

Dear Ones, Hope of God:

It is hoped that this letter finds you in good spirit and in good health. In the letters which have reached me during these past few weeks, I see that there are some serious questions about beginning work.

There are three main lines of work for the beginner in which one can store up a great deal of work material for later when one is able to make inner world change.

First – One can learn to accept displeasing manifestations originating in others and in the environment without becoming either inwardly or outwardly agitated or resentful. This provides real material useful for "fanning the sparks of the purifying fire" which fuses the centers into a unified entity.

Second – One can perform one's daily tasks with extreme and powerful attention. In this way one forms material for later work in self-observation and makes a basis for inner exercises which can be added to ordinary tasks.

Third – One can learn to surpass the ordinary limits of the organism, mind beliefs and attitudes. Thus one forces the ordinary centers of gravity of the personality to seek new sources of energy...Possibly to tap the force of the Power Center, which under ordinary circumstances does not come into play.

In one letter which came a few days ago the question was asked: "Is it possible to make small temporary change in essence without inner effort?" In order to answer this question seriously it is first necessary to take a little time to view the underlying factors which make this possible.

As you are quite aware, the psyche is a mechanical and artificial device which makes possible the operation of the organism without any participation on the part of the essence.

Thus the psyche is the substitute for what should be the real operator of the organism.

Just how this state of affairs came about is the subject for much more than a letter, but suffice it to say that it happened more or less to every human being on the planet Earth.

On the other hand, essence, although ordinarily not in control of, or responsible for, the manifestations of the being, is that part of a man which can be said to be genuine. This deep self is not a real identity, however. As it exists presently, it is nothing more than an accidental accumulation of tendencies and habits.

While the psyche is lodged in the mind, nervous system and skin, the essence is represented by the muscle system.

Although some changes can be made in the behavior through the mind, perceptions and emotions, no real inner change can be made through these ordinary channels of access.

There is a very good reason to make a change in essence…For instance to help someone past a barrier they otherwise could not overcome. Even though the change is temporary, it may give the boost needed.

If one understands that the essence has no possibility of formulating an aim, and that only by giving an outer aim is it possible to form a "temporary magnetic center" one will understand the use of this method I am about to introduce to you.

A small, temporary change in essence can be made through the muscles. This alteration can be made artificially with the use of radical posture change combined with certain techniques of massage. Since these are induced from external causes and not through continual practice, they do not make a lasting change.

In some cases such a change is necessary, as for instance in the case of drug addicts and alcoholics, who need a respite before beginning longer-term therapeutic treatment.

Over a longer period of time one may make permanent changes through the muscle system with the use of gymnastic and rhythmic exercises combined with inner mental and emotional exercises designed for that individual. In order to do this, however, one must know exactly which changes to make.

If one understands the application of this method and the exact changes necessary for conscious life, along with the understanding of the laws of world creation and maintenance, development of conscience, objective obligation, the means for the collection of salts and their transformation into higher substances, crystallization of the higher being bodies and law- conformability... Hmmm... It just now has occurred to me that there may, as many have said before me, be more about this than can be conveyed in letters.

Perhaps it would be wiser to wait until we are able to work together in person. There will be time then to make all the experiments and ask all the questions you might wish. Until then, I will refrain from wise-acring about such serious matters and tend strictly to my business here. No more letters for the moment. Enough!

THE ETHICS

Gaia takes a selfie

We should occupy ourselves in trade, commerce and crafts. To be in the Work does not excuse us from earning our own livelihood. We owe first responsibility to our family; our first effort should be to provide our planetary body with its immediate necessities.

To be poor just for the sake of piousness is pathological. Only when one fears objects does one fear temptation. Complete understanding of the power of identification with objects results in placing little or no faith in anything or anyone of the outer world. But at the same time, one must try to love everything that breathes.

Heaven and Hell are not results of what we do in life, but of identification with the dream.

While Saints are constrained to conceal their activities, Messengers From Above are required to reveal themselves.

One who has Reason is able to discriminate between the seduction of amusement and the inspiration of Truth.

Some who come to the school are overcome by grief; some by yearning; some by sadness; still others by hope. All these are simply burdens carried in from the dream. Conditioning is burned away through friction and self-remembering.

Sentimentality is a luxury we cannot afford in ourselves if we wish to make a place for ourselves in the New World.

The secret for you now is to try always to behave in accordance with the objective customs of hospitality. To do this, one must first learn what these customs are.

Those attending meetings may be in several states: inspired with love, inspired with hope, or inspired with faith. Each of these in ordinary man can be turned into its opposite lower emotion. Love into hate, hope into despair, faith into fear. We must not allow our lower emotions to rule us. We must hold ourselves above psychopathy.

We should learn the laws of cosmic harmony and become law-conformable to them, but should remain inwardly free in order to be able to take hazard for the sake of truth.

Pupils can be divided into three main categories; Saints, who understand how to be a reconciling force for those on both sides of the law; Scholars, who are attached to the form of the law; and Objective Scientists, who understand law only in relation to the understanding of mutuality, action or nonaction, and idiotism.

It should not be our way to seek exotic understanding of laws, nor to pervert them in order to justify our lower nature desires.

In the outer school we are given historical data. In the middle school, exercises to know how to know. In the inner school it is up to us to find answers to our questions, and to find questions to our answers.

The school has both internal and external effects. The external is to observe customs and bow to the king in the outer world. The inner is to make all quiet inside and to prepare the soil for the collection of higher substances for the formation of a soul.

Each state, experience and initiation has its own subjective responsibility and its own objective obligation.

Some people are identified with the dream, some with religion, some with the school. Identification is still identification, no matter what.

Morality depends upon language, history, literature, custom and conditioning. Conscience depends upon an understanding of objective suffering.

The least we are asked to be able to do as completed man is to suffer the unpleasant manifestations of others toward ourselves and others without resentment, to take no action against wrongs done us, and to have compassion for those whose nature is more powerful than their being.

States are a form of inspiration. To observe our states is to observe ourselves being breathed.

When we first come to the school we control our manifestations with the help of inhibitions. After a while our manifestations become our master. We must find a way to become master.

We should learn to associate with beings of every type, especially those we cannot tolerate, in order to have every possible kind of impression.

Learn to endure momentary displeasures for the sake of the Work.

We should not inflict our understanding on new pupils, but should wait until asked for help.

Fellowship in the Work requires agreement on everything lawful.

Ego depends on belief in an unlimited future.

To worship one's inner evil god is what is meant by self-love.

Make friends with the denying force.

If we are doubtful as to which course to follow, we should follow the line of most resistance.

One who endues the unconsciousness of others is closer to the Work than one who shuts himself up in a monastery.

We should respect the teacher and his work, acting as much as possible from conscience.

We should remember that the teacher is consciously the denying force for our questions. We must overcome his resistance and find a way to use him as he could be used.

To become strong we must learn to be gentle.

Do not follow the customs of sleeping men.

Patanjali takes a selfie

The Ethics of Hospitality

We should give a guest whatever food or drink we have reserved for ourselves.

Even if we have little, we should not be ashamed, nor should a guest despise what is offered in hospitality.

Hospitality is the greatest law given to man. If he knew how to obey this one law, he could overcome his imperfections.

We must accept hospitality if offered, and not avoid offering it to others.

A guest ceases to be a guest on the fourth day of his visit, and only then may he be asked to join in work for the household or community.

If one does not have food in one's house for a guest, one must meet him outside one's home.

One should not force oneself to accept a guest one cannot treat with honor.

Aphrodite takes a selfie

The Ethics of Wandering

He can only be an aristocrat who asks where you are taking him when you invite him to walk with you.

Travel is a way of self-discipline.

One should not travel just for amusement.

If one has companions, one should serve them whenever possible.

When entering a city, one should visit the sanctuary.

When entering sanctuary, one should take off one's shoes left shoe first, before entering and in reverse order when leaving, then wash in the water provided at the door, and bow twice with hands folded at the heart. Only after this is he ready to enter the space and to greet those within it. If there is a teacher present, he should kiss the head, but of the guest is a novice, he should kiss his hand instead.

When visiting with a teacher one should sit for a while without speaking except when asked a question. During this time tea or coffee may be served. If a toast is made with wine or cognac, one is obligated to honor it.

If the teacher offers food or drink, it may not be refused. If the teacher is equal in rank to the teacher, he may talk freely. One who needs knowledge of another should not dwell upon his faults.

Fatima takes a selfie

The Ethics of Awakening

After the first momentary awakening from the dream, one should seek a guide who will teach one the rights and obligations of a candidate for the Work.

If a seed is not planted in soil it will not germinate.

For the rose to live, the seed must die.

The novice is the seed. He will not survive transformation.

The conditions of the school create the possibility for the seed to die.

Refusal to activate the impulses of remorse and organic shame is more serious than failure to perform sacred vows. One may still repent until the closing of the Gate of Seven Veils.

When the seeker attains all stations and has mastered each one according to its measure, he is entitled to wear the robe. If he takes the robe he must observe all obligations attached to the mantle. Before this he should have tamed his nature through the tests of each station.

The seeker should be able to recognize his faults without identifying with them. He must be able to control his animal nature by mental exertion and by examination of conscience.

The seeker must never refuse to carry out an exercise or instruction if given by the guide.

The seeker should follow the stations without impatience to get to the next one before the present one has been mastered.

One should work with full attention, striving to become active in essence and passive in psyche.

When one abstains from actions of form, only then will he be free of the world.

To render service and hospitality is more valuable than to be engaged in prayer for oneself.

Only if one can do for oneself should one try to do for another.

It is said that the student should not leave his teacher until the heart can see, he can listen to the moment, and obey the Law.

Ghost takes a selfie

The Ethics of Discourse

The purpose of discourse is to guide the questioner to the space in which he is alone.

In order to attain to the right to receive an answer to any question he asks, a candidate must prove willingness to answer any question, regardless of his state at the moment.

The novice should only ask those questions which reflect present necessity.

Knowledge may only be transmitted in Sanctuary.

Wisdom of the Sanctuary is not for the dream.

One should always try to speak in front of the wise, for the ignorant will not correct ignorance.

It is always permitted to teach to any who ask.

There is knowledge from God, knowledge about God, and knowledge which is God.

He who listens with his ears will tell what he has heard; he who listens with his heart will preach; but only he who listens with all his being is able to guide.

The teacher depends upon a questioner to bring with him his own discernment and his own common sense.

While in Sanctuary, the guest should not inquire about worldly matters, but only those things pertaining to work of Sanctuary.

He who takes no care for stylish appearance and who has no care for one food or drink over another is welcomed as a brother in Sanctuary.

Sphynx takes a selfie

Instructions For Sanctuary

If you are in this room, and you know you are in this room, you are awake.

The work of the work group is "to do nothing".

Reach out actively for the words spoken in Sanctuary, rather than let them come to you passively.

Do not pass on to others outside Sanctuary what has been given in Sanctuary.

Surrender to the space of Sanctuary.

Work to refine your questions. In Sanctuary everything is taken literally.

Make no effort to get money for the school. The flow of baraka takes care of all the school's needs.

Do not bring people to the school, nor advertise for students. When the Sanctuary is open, those who should come to it come to it.

If someone belongs in the Sanctuary, nothing you say will convince them to leave. If they do not belong there, nothing you say will convince them to stay.

Do not expend Power-Center energy within the dream. Conserve it for work within the Sanctuary.

The Sanctuary in its prototype-form is the teaching itself.

Do not bring garments from the dream world into Sanctuary.

Assume your post as it is in the archetype. The closer to the archetype every object in the room can be brought, the easier it is to upscale to the archetype.

Only by understanding the function of the dream are you able to understand how it is possible to leave Sanctuary and go into the dream without ever having left Sanctuary.

Zeus takes a selfie

The Ethics of Sanctuary

The Meeting in Sanctuary is inspiration of truth. He who breathes it in truth will realize it in truth, while he who hears it with the lusts of his animal soul will only hear his own conditioning.

It is a rule that candidates do not behave in an affected manner during the Meeting in Sanctuary, and that they not attend for the purpose of being entertained.

It is said that to make one error in Meeting is worse that to commit crimes in the dream world.

It is forbidden to induce an artificial state of ecstasy or to rise and dance during Meeting. But if a guest does so, everyone must do as he does so that he is not embarrassed in his ignorance or lack of self-discipline.

To remain quiet, yet attentive, is best. To make all quiet inside is one of the foremost admonitions of the work space.

Ganesh takes a selfie

The Ethics of Eating

One should give to guests from one's own bowl.

One should say before each mouthful, "I had nothing but myself with which to create the world; out of myself the world was made."

One should say at the beginning of each meal, "I wish to remember myself," at the same time holding in mind the image of Sanctuary.

One should partake of food as if it were medicine. Those who have passed the first six stations may dispense with this rule.

Dissolve food by repeating the Great Mantra and by revealing to yourself the nature of all food.

No one should say to another, "Eat this food," unless it is the teacher, who may do this to encourage a shy guest at his table.

The kitchen is the center of work; the table the receptive to the Grace of God; and Sanctuary is the source of their power.

When one eats in company he should not withdraw from the table before the others.

When asked what kind of food was unlawful, one teacher answered, "Any food you cannot refuse from desire."

One may not return food presented to him as a guest. A guest is only entitled to dispose of food by ingestion.

Tibetan God takes a selfie

The Ethics of Sleep

Sleep is regenerative; guilt should not be associated with it.

Prolonged sleep is not the custom of the wise.

One should not lie down to sleep while in the company of people who are seated.

Sleep is intended to provide energy for work in Sanctuary.

THE SACRIFICES

Apollo takes a selfie

0

THE SACRIFICE
OF PEACE OF MIND

The first sacrifice ordinary man cannot make for himself...another must make it for him. This is why the first sacrifice is numbered zero. The Sacrifice of Peace of Mind is brought about simply by being exposed to the possibility of knowledge, thus having the opportunity for transformation.

In the diagram of certain alchemical processes there is usually shown a cave into which the experimenter is entering. He is expected to go all the way through to the other end of the cave.

This cave is also called "The Labyrinth." We call it the Corridor of Madness. It is the period during which the psyche is "eaten" by the essence – when the impressions stored in the false centers are transferred to the real essence centers. After this, essence emerges as the active – rather than the passive – force controlling the organism.

The corridor must be traversed completely from one end to the other without stopping, going off in search of side exits, turning back or hoping for outside help. We must not give in to despair, or look for something soothing and calming within the corridor. This is the real meaning of the magician's warning to Aladdin (Al' Uddin) in the cave of treasures

Nothing other than the path of struggle will be effective in the corridor. The madness will not abate until the end has been reached. This is why essence is exposed and tested before the student begins his journey. If essence is too fearful, savage or stupid – or if it holds its own survival at the cost of other beings – it is not allowed to embark on the journey under the guidance of the school at that time. One is never allowed to endanger the Work.

Athena takes a selfie

I

THE SACRIFICE
OF COMFORT

Life of Austerity

Our own comfort prevents us from seeing where we may work and serve. Comfort can be deceptive – it may be material, mental, spiritual. We may uncover one teacher and school after another, compare their company, wander in the world from place to place seeking the unusual and the miraculous all for our own comfort without recognizing it as the search for comfort.

We may surround ourselves with the comforts of our lives – friends, parents, family and home – whether it be rich or poor, in the struggle to maintain the familiar surroundings of our fathers, cocooned by the buffers of everyday life, cut off by complacency and disinterest form our world and the full potential of our beings.

To make this sacrifice we live an austere life, disciplined and clean. Surrounded by no objects by which one can attach oneself or amuse oneself we are confronted by the continuous presence of the deepest self.

Our life is exactly regulated in periods of service, devotions, Sdaily work for the community of the school, personal needs, and household routines.

There is no unnecessary talking or whispering, no horseplay or entertainment. One avoids excesses of pleasure in all things. To every activity there are limits in the amount needed. We find and remain within those limits in sleep, food, talking, studying, work, play, and other personal functions.

One dresses simply, in a non-egoistic manner, keeping personal and household cleanliness to a fault. In walking, breathing, eating, waking and sleeping we are responsible for the regulation and manifestations of body and psyche.

We monitor our feelings, inner agitations, attitudes, and perceptions with full attention during work, never allowing ourselves a public display of our inner life activities.

In daily service one is obligated to perform continuous ritual observances both day and night, with short rest periods in between.

We study the Sacred Scriptures whenever there is a brief period, which allows for it. We practice complete celibacy at this time in order to provide a basis for high states of energy in the ordinary centers.

There are continual exercises, both group and personal designed for individuals to help overcome barriers to work.

The work required for household and community maintenance is performed carefully and with extreme attention, paced rapidly or slowly as required to root the attention to the task at hand through a change of tempo of activity.

The diet is simple and austere, although unappetizing. It is a high-quality food substance, but low in quantity and pleasurable sensations. One should feel slightly hungry after having just eaten, and must then depend upon air as a second source of food, and results of impressions as a third source.

Of course special care is taken for dietary problems. Special consideration is given to those who cannot yet come to this sacrifice. Our own solution to this is to have those who cannot make this sacrifice remain in study groups until they feel able and willing to endure it.

Ordinary efforts are useless in work, and one must make only great efforts in order to overcome the comfort of inertia. Only by making such efforts is it possible to overcome the tendency to remain calm.

One must decide once and for all to surrender oneself to the discipline of the school and the teacher without hesitation – or future betrayal – of this self-surrender.

One is expected to wage a continual struggle against the Dominant Habit, and to welcome any chance given by the teacher or other pupils for this effort. In the Sacrifice of Comfort one must consciously choose the Path of Struggle, and actively seek from the teacher all possible tasks, efforts and interpersonal frictions which produce potential for self-struggle.

One must work with all centers of the whole being, learning always to work with attention, will and effort.

One is expected to be receptive by keeping silence – not all the time, but when it counts. On the other hand, one must not expect anything in return for one's efforts.

One must never speak of love in connection with the work until one has passed beyond the level of sentimentality.

One endures everything and everyone in silence, suffering in restraint by always attaching to this the intention of work. There is no better beginning method than this effort.

Shiva takes a selfie

II

THE SACRIFICE
OF DESIRES

Life of Humility

How is it possible to sacrifice one's desires without having first sacrificed one's comfort? Only after having done so, this second sacrifice becomes possible.

In the Sacrifice of Desires we become last in all things, making continual efforts to perform tasks without resentment, inner agitation, and particularly without pride in being of service. Pride of service is without doubt the most insidious potential trap on this level, and one who does not watch for it with fierce attention is doomed to continue to make this sacrifice for a long time.

One may perform menial tasks for the community, such as maintaining the fire – an important job – which is kept continually during periods of sacrifice. One may also clean and maintain the unpleasing parts of the household, such as the kitchen and toilet and dining room. These areas may occasionally be scrubbed down from top to bottom every hour or two.

One shows humility in all things and has the least importance in the household or in the work. One must outwardly at least be respectful to all other members of the community on whatever level they may be.

One must accept all corrections of one's attitudes, behavior, or actions, whether true or not in one's own opinion, and one is polite to the extreme – without being groveling or obsequious. One shows courtesy to others by recognizing the essence within them. That is to say, one always bows deeply whenever addressed by another member of the community of work. One does not speak unless spoken to, and one never comments or complains. At this all-important stage, one seeks help rather than offering it.

Here one functions as a caretaker for the personal needs of others but not for oneself. One is more concerned that the other members of the community may do their work without having to worry over daily necessities, and tries to make their lives easier by eliminating ordinary obstacles for them by doing for them all manner of unpleasant or menial things.

One serves the Obligatory Sacred Observances by cleaning and caring for the area where the said observances are held. If one studies this function closely, one can see that it literally requires one to work with profound attention.

In the kitchen one serves as a helper but not as cook – eating whatever has been left over after the meal. But in this case one must not put aside food for oneself. Usually one's diet will consist of cold and unwanted food, or nothing at all.

Sebek takes a selfie

III

THE SACRIFICE
OF HABITS

Life of the Contrary

Why should one sacrifice one's habits? Almost everyone understands this in an ordinary way.

But there is another more important facet to this. The nature of the Corridor of Madness is such that one is left with the identity and ability to take action in the present only with habits. One could say that in the deepest self, one is nothing but habits, for only habits survive transition. One cannot depend upon the psyche, which provides the mind, body, memory, decision-making apparatus, ordinary good-bad and like-dislike attitudes, forms of consciousness and sense of identity.

Without these, one is left with . . . What? Only habits – and how can one remain awake with habits which are in themselves unconscious and which always in everything will choose unconscious life? We can demonstrate this. It is the body of habits, called the essence, that forms a psyche, allowing it to dominate the organism, make decisions, take actions, and control the organism throughout one's ordinary life. This demonstrates the lazy nature of essence if it is composed of unconsciously accumulated habits and not consciously created ones.

The nature of the Transit State is such that one can remain awake throughout the series of events in order to consciously choose one's path. It is not possible to "accidentally fall into" the Path of Struggle, as many wish to believe.

One's habit of falling asleep and giving responsibility for the Self to the psyche – or automatic machinery of a false identity – must be overcome before one enters the Corridor of Madness – the Transit State. Otherwise one will surely rebuild the psyche – ordinary consciousness – once again, and one is destined to live out yet another life in the same way. This cycle of repetition cannot be broken by ordinary effort.

As the essence develops, it "eats" the psyche little by little, just as the yolk of an egg depends upon the albumen. Thus the psyche is not destroyed utterly. Its hold over the essence is broken, and its domination of the organism is finished.

As this occurs, one approaches the door – marked "Unknown" – and indeed, not only unknown, but unknowable – which stands before the Corridor of Madness, through which the psyche is completely broken down and absorbed. At the end the essence emerges, freshly born without complexity.

The primary habit one can approach at this time, and with which one has genuine and not just imaginary power, is the habit of creating a psyche with which to handle life automatically.

IV

THE SACRIFICE
OF ORDINARY LIFE

Life of the Unclean

One sacrifices ordinary life, only to return to it after having become changed. But although one returns to it, one sacrifices ordinary life forever, because having become changed, one has transcended everything which makes the world powerful. One can say that the world no longer has authority over one's essence nature. It loses its power of fascination.

To sacrifice one's ordinary life one must dress badly – even stupidly – and keep a slovenly, yet clean, appearance. One wears torn clothing, walks with a shuffle, appears to be lazy and incompetent – even dangerously so.

But while one seems stupid to others, one performs all tasks with attention and powerful intention, and one remembers one's aim to work on oneself, attaching that idea to all manifestations, decisions, reactions, and relationships.

In short, one becomes "unclean" only in appearance, but not in one's inner life or duties to the community of work.

One is restricted from attending all Sacred Observances and Obligatories. One may not read, study, or discuss the Sacred Scriptures or efforts for work with others. One is isolated from the work community and treated as if unclean. One is not permitted to perform household tasks or temple duties either for the work community or for an outside community. One becomes a complete outsider.

One may not eat at the table with others, walk into or through the kitchen area, dining area or temple, handle food or eating utensils used by others, clean eating areas or walk through places used for the carrying on of work in assimilating or studying.

One may not handle food substances used by others or make offerings of any kind during or between obligatories. One must in fact be literally spoon-fed by another who is now in the stage of service, so that the utensil will not be touched by one's hands.

One may only be addressed by one's teacher or by one's server during this stage. Even the coach or assistant to the teacher are forbidden to communicate with one who is unclean.

Mut takes a selfie

V

THE SACRIFICE
OF TENDENCIES

Life of Ritual

When we are with an individual who is in the Corridor of Madness, we must be able to be with that individual continually, without falling asleep. In the Corridor of Madness it is not a matter of what one does or knows, but of remaining awake throughout the experience.

One must learn to be constant to the task or work – this is something which must be cultivated within oneself. It is the imaginary ability that holds one down, for it prevents the real ability from being developed.

Keeping oneself or another awake is like the passenger in the automobile who must keep the driver alert on a long and seemingly endless journey. One may sing, tell stories, or poke him – one does for him whatever is possible.

To make this sacrifice one lives a completely ritualized existence, making all Obligatory Observances and Purifications.

One wears vestments at all times, and eats only special food which has been dedicated and blessed. One sits in the temple while eating. Food is taken within the sanctuary of the Holy Ark. One performs vigil with this food. Sleep, dress, eating, movement and toilet are all performed as ritual purifications. One is obligated only to perform rituals and may not work for the household in ordinary tasks.

Kali takes a selfie

VI

THE SACRIFICE
OF CONTROL

Life of Passivity

Now one learns to give up control not only of one's ordinary manifestations such as "fidgeting" physically, mentally and emotionally, but one must also give up all control of others, of the environment, of attempts to influence others through action, drama, or emotional ploys. One must give up all imaginary powers in order to achieve even a small measure of freedom.

To make the sacrifice of control, one allows all one's actions to be directed by another who is responsible for one during this stage.

This includes all actions, waking or sleeping. Even one's toilet must be guided to some degree by another. One behaves as if totally helpless and unable to do even the smallest thing. One allows another to guide one in everything until the desire for control dies away.

One is carried on a litter to obligatories and allowed to take part only passively. One eats and drinks in the same way, and makes no choice even by sign of preferences about food, drink, action, rest, or areas to which one may be taken during the day.

When one emerges from the Corridor of Madness, one will be left helpless as a newborn babe, except that one will be able to do only those things which one is able to do with one's muscles – but these abilities in the muscles must be habitual with one. If one has not prepared oneself with handcrafts, movements and mime, one must be prepared to accept this temporary condition of utter helplessness.

Why should one prepare in this way if one is now making muscle preparations with handicrafts and movement? Because one cannot be sure these have become habitual until the essence emerges from the Corridor stripped of the psyche. But by then, it is too late to do anything except either endure helplessness or enjoy the ability to do.

Vishnu takes a selfie

VII

THE SACRIFICE
OF RELATIONSHIPS

Life of Arrogance

To make this sacrifice one does everything as if one already knows everything and has nothing to learn. Many are already making this difficult sacrifice, but a little too soon...

One gives unwanted and unasked for advice to others continually, ridicules and doubts everyone and everything, even while protesting innocence. One always and in everything takes the superior attitude.

One behaves as the "Keeper of Integrity" for all the others. Taking no real part in the action, one observes the others who keep the rituals and then later critiques them for "right" and "wrong" actions.

At this stage one is first in all things – one may take a large and special portion as one wishes during meals and one may always have one's way over the will of another student during a confrontation.

One may at this time do whatever one wishes during the day, taking part or not taking part in obligatories, household duties, community work or any other work of the school. If one does undertake a task at this stage, it must be as a supervisor and not as a worker. One may not "soil one's hands" at menial toil, even if before one had been a ranch hand or worker in a boiler factory.

One is now treated as an "honored guest", Elisha, and is shown deep respect and humility by the others. One is always right in every matter and another may not point our "errors" about one even by inflection, tone, gesture, expression or inner emotions.

Patanjali takes a selfie

VIII

*THE SACRIFICE
OF ONE'S
PLACE IN THE WORK*

Life of Outer Freedom

One must now leave the work for a specific, stated and known interval. One may do no practice of any kind, nor may one have open contact with anyone in the work during this period. One is considered unable to accept help of any kind. One needs to learn from oneself at this stage. One must be able to work through this dilemma of no active part in the work by oneself, without outside help. Then if one wishes to return, one may again address the remainder of the sacrifices if one is still able and willing to continue.

Buddha takes a selfie

IX

THE SACRIFICE
OF SANITY

Life of Essence

Now one goes through the door of the Corridor of Madness. What is madness? It is the undeveloped essence forcefully exploded into the active role of controlling the organism, which up to then had been under the command of the psyche.

It appears as if a three-year-old has suddenly been put in charge. Sometimes it seems as if one has forgotten everything, even how to think and act.

Essence is very simple. It consists of only a very few habits and no more. The essence, unlike the psyche, does not find life difficult or complex. There are few needs, if any. Desires, aims, achieving, social life, artistic striving, politics, explanations, conversation – all the ordinary aspects of the psyche – have fallen away.

One's action and speech is taken from the environment and not from within. Feeling and sensing are taken from within, not from the environment. In short, one learns to think with one's feelings.

One always speaks about oneself in third person as an object. The self is the psyche and the "I" is the essence. One practices by giving the teaching to one's food before ingestion, by treating food as a living being with full consciousness and awareness, who needs and deserves to receive the Method before final assimilation.

One approaches each task from the point of view of the needs and consciousness of the outer world environment. One gives running commentary and instruction to the body as if to a computer and machine not directly connected to one's control center, but able to hear and to obey verbal or thought commands.

One behaves as if one is the commander of a ship and addresses the body and mind as if they were the crew. One assumes an unattached viewpoint in which one is able to issue directions and instructions for the actions of the body and mind.

One may say; "Now it is going over to the stove. Now it is turning on the gas . . . Now it is reaching for a pan...." But one never says; "Now I am going over to the stove."

There are barriers to the Corridor of Madness, just as the Corridor of Madness is a barrier to the work itself. One may encounter money, attitudes, fears, endurance, impossible teachers, personal interests, the ridicule of others, or fears, as barriers which remain insurmountable if one is the least unsure of one's aim in taking the dangerous journey through the Corridor.

Should one resist madness when in the Corridor, one is sure to be overcome by the visions of darkness. There are no side doors or exits except the one exit at the end of the tunnel.

As one first enters the corridor, one may see some of the things ahead, and may not want to continue. In this case one must immediately and without hesitation leave the work. This is the last time it is safe to leave the work, and if one continues but does not endure to the end, one will never attain sleep comfortably or soundly.

The madness will not abate even for an instant until the end of the corridor has been reached. This warning is always given before one enters. One can never say that one was not told of the dangers before the journey.

Devi takes a selfie

X

THE SACRIFICE
OF CONSCIOUSNESS

Life of Incoherence

To make this sacrifice one simply becomes like a babbling idiot, dressing and behaving so stupidly that he forgets his own grandmother and she wishes now to forget him also.

The Great Betrayal – the moment at which the child decided that life was too complex to meet with the simple essence, and allowed outside influences to form a psyche, must now be found, met face to face, understood, and absorbed.

XI

THE SACRIFICE
OF THE GURU

Life of Hopelessness

One lives as the Guru and receives homage and respect as the embodiment of the Great Guide. One must neither inwardly nor outwardly break the role during this stage. One gathers disciples cheerfully and dispenses Grace according to objective merit and impartial justice. One becomes the Guru, thus sacrificing the outer help of another.

Avalokiteshvara takes a selfie

XII

THE SACRIFICE
OF EXISTENCE

Ordinary Life

At this stage one returns to the practices given in the Sacrifice of Comfort, the first stage of Real Work. The work schedule takes up one's entire day. The only difference is that now one may give service outside the community of work. One may take the role of teacher, allowing the Method to channel through oneself for the benefit of others.

Nataraja takes a selfie

XIII

THE SACRIFICE
OF HEALTH

Super Life

In this stage one learns to make super-powerful efforts, because it is understood that the ordinary centers can only be burned away through the use of super-energies, when the Power Center is in use beyond the level of ordinary effort.

The energies of the Power Center will also be needed to drive the bigger and more active Higher Centers – the results of the fusion of the lower ordinary centers common to human beings before work on self.

Through super-effort one is able to arouse the huge accumulator of the Power Center, thus enabling the teacher to direct this energy to the ordinary centers of thinking, feeling, sensing, moving, and automatic organic control. In this way they can be fused into a single permanent identity, making food for the essence as it grows into Real Beingness. Now essence will be able to remain exposed and in control of the organism – responsible for itself – for the first time in life.

The higher bodies must pass through all three stages of formation: Fusion, Perfection, and Crystallization. Should the salts of the new higher being body form incorrectly, rather than allow it to crystallize as immortal, the higher body is broken down – through great suffering – and rebuilt from the beginning.

Hanuman takes a selfie

XIV

THE SACRIFICE
OF HEART

Life of Redemption

It is here that one gathers the will, ability and knowledge to free the centers from slavery to the psyche.

The Thinking Center becomes the higher center, the Center of Understanding. The Emotional Center becomes in its higher state the Feeling Center. The Moving Center and seat of sensations becomes the higher center, the Center of Co-Creation, in which one creates co-motion with the universe, aligning one's own wishes with the universal will. The Center of Automatic Functions becomes in its higher state the Center of Being. With these higher centers in operation, one is now able to be, to feel, to do, and to sense the whole of oneself.

In order to accomplish this seemingly easy task, it will be necessary to first sacrifice one's beliefs, emotions, feelings, thinking and ordinary compassion – all those imaginary properties of ordinary man – in order to move into the field of Love itself. While within this magnetic field of Pure Love one becomes Love itself, a catalyst, not an element, and so one cannot experience Love itself as an independently existing force. The catalyst, while profoundly affecting other elements, undergoes no change of its own during interaction in changing other elements from physical combination to chemical fusion.

Grim Reaper takes a selfie

XV

THE SACRIFICE
OF HOPE

Life of Nothingness

Here one sees the utter reality of endlessness and nothingness and realizes that there is no permanent and eternal attainment in an ordinary way. One resolves to make a permanent change only in that which exists beyond the laws of infinity and eternity.

One turns one's own hopes for oneself into compassion for all beings – those left behind during the personal struggle for freedom. Now one returns to the prison, exempt from its suffering, perhaps to lead a few prisoners in the escape. Even so, one realizes that there can never be a "Great Escape" from this prison, and that the majority are forever destined to feed the Void at the Point of New Creation.

Sarada Devi takes a selfie

XVI

THE SACRIFICE
OF SELF-PITY

Life of Benevolence

Until one is actually able to help others, one cannot hope to attain Real Benevolence. Compassion alone is not sufficient – one must also have ability, so that compassion is transformed into mercy.

In this stage one learns the relationship between the movements and the aphorisms – the language of The Dance – and begins to transmit and read through choreography the fragments of truth necessary to future generations.

One learns to encode and decode the Method through movement, architecture, painting, sculpture, music, and dance; those fragments which may be lost otherwise during ages to come through accidental loss, warfare, or as a result of superstition and fear. One learns the language of relativity, or ratios, becoming an Objective Mathematician.

Horus takes a selfie

XVII

THE SACRIFICE
OF SUFFERING AND
DESPAIR

Life of Awakening

Now one transcends the Fourth and Fifth Bodies developed through the sacrifices of hope, self-pity and sacred obligation. One begins to intentionally develop mental powers, or siddhis, over the material universe. In this effort one is forced to pass beyond the barrier of sentimentality into the realm of impartial justice and the beginnings of conscience.

One learns how to replace unconscious habits with habits leading automatically and perpetually to conscious life.

It is here that one's will, attention, and mental powers are developed to the fullest. One may now attempt to transmit to others the Method as one understands it so far, and may use one's Magnetic Force of Attraction to bring pupils under the influence of the school. When necessary, it is permitted to use one's powers to save a life, perform experiments with the forcible division of psyche and essence, or to create energies for work. Without full development of this potential, fusion of the Seventh Body is not possible.

Isis takes a selfie

XVIII

THE SACRIFICE
OF REDEMPTION

Life of Stillness

In this stage one prepares the groundwork or foundation for the development of the conscience. One gives up all powers of the Sixth Body, thus destroying all previous attainments. One relies upon nothing whatever to make things "happen" or "go right". One reaches the crossroads where the choice is given to graft oneself to the Body of Power or to gamble everything for the attainment of permanent conscious life.

During this stage one must remain in this helpless condition in which one is played upon by nature and by accidental circumstances – the Laws of Coincidence. One must not even for a moment use one's former powers, even though they are still available. Should one do so, one must begin all over again.

If one should succeed in attaining the Seventh Body, one has reached the limit of attainment possible in this universe for a human being. Beyond this, one must be in a new form of space, time and beingness in which to go past these human and superhuman limits.

After one has passed this stage one may again choose to apply the powers for the good of others. But even if one's closest is dying, one may not use them during this period of testing. For one who is in the midst of the development of the Seventh Body – the Harmonious Human Being – everything must be done in an ordinary way.

It is during this stage that everything will seem to go wrong – that the universe will conspire against one's work. One's very vulnerability will attract the victimizers and the violent.

It does not become easier as one approaches the end, it gets worse, much worse. And this, the Last Temptation, will seem the hardest barrier of all – because it is so easy to fall for just one moment. But at the end of the corridor, "thirty birds" await your arrival.

Krishna takes a selfie

E.J. Gold – Author Biography

E.J. Gold has been a prominent and controversial figure in the Human Potential movement in California for over 45 years. Technically a "shamanic rabbi", he earned respect in the field of transformational psychology by the clarity, profundity, uniqueness and expertise of his writings and thoughts and his emphasis on a practical approach towards transformation.

He has written dozens of books in his field with wide-ranging subjects, from attention and presence; the waking versus sleeping state; death and dying; to shamanism; interdimensional voyaging; artifact reading, imprinting and use; cosmic laws; the suffering of the Absolute; higher bodies; artistic expression; the Tarot; prayer; shakti; natural childbirth; and many more themes. He is recognized as an authority in many of these areas, but death and dying will always be central to his vision, explorations and projects.

Angels Healing Journey is one of several powerful texts he has written to help those interested in healing and working with people going through transition, including the final passage out of this life. His best-known book, the *American Book of the Dead*, is a modern Western version of the *Bardo Thodol*, or *Tibetan Book of the Dead*, that has sold over 200,000 copies and been translated into several other languages. It was reprinted by Harper SanFrancisco in 1995.

Described as a teacher's teacher, his influence and association with contemporaries includes Timothy Leary, Dr. John Lilly, Rabbi Zalman Schachter, Robert Anton Wilson, Dr. Claudio Naranjo, Swami Vishnu Devananda, Chogyam Trungpa, Dr. Fritz Perls, Elisabeth Kubler-Ross, Reshad Feild, Tarthang Tulku Rinpoche, Heather Valencia, Robert de Ropp, Joan Halifax, Paul Anderson, Antonio Asin, and many others.

In spite of all these associations and his remarkable list of accomplishments, Gold has preferred to maintain a high level of privacy and isolation from the media. However, he has become very active on the internet, especially since the pandemic years of 2020-21. He meets with students in zoom and has spent years in certain gaming platforms where he is a veteran. Over the past decade he has been developing his own computer game, G.O.D.D., to enable players to experience and work with the bardo.

Gold attributes much of his skill as a writer and versatility as a transformational psychologist and consciousness explorer to his culturally privileged background. As the son of H.L. Gold, the famous writer and founding editor of Galaxy Science Fiction Magazine, he grew up surrounded by writers such as Isaac Asimov, Frank Herbert, Robert Heinlein, Arthur C. Clarke, Harlan Ellison, to name a few. Other family friends included John Cage, Ben Shahn, Julian Huxley, Orson Welles, Merce Cunningham, Charles Laughton and Elsa Lanchester.

Dear Reader,

If you find this book useful, we encourage you to explore the books you will find at our website:

www.gatewaysbooksandtapes.com

If you are interested in the work of E.J. Gold and the community of IDHHB, visit

http://idhhb.com/

or Prosperity Path Forum on Facebook:

https://www.facebook.com/search/top/?q=prosperity %20path.

We can also be reached by phone:

(800) 869-0658 or (530) 271-2239

or by mail:

IDHHB, Inc.
P.O. Box 370
Nevada City, Ca. 95959

Sincerely,
The Editors
Gateways Books and Tapes